FOCUS ON
MEXICO

CELIA TIDMARSH

WORLD ALMANAC® LIBRARY

Please visit our web site at: www.worldalmanaclibrary.com
For a free color catalog describing World Almanac® Library's list of high-quality books and multimedia programs, call 1-800-848-2928 (USA) or 1-800-387-3178 (Canada). World Almanac® Library's fax: (414) 332-3567.

Library of Congress Cataloging-in-Publication Data available upon request from publisher. Fax (414) 336-0157 for the attention of the Publishing Records Department.

ISBN 0-8368-6219-8 (lib. bdg.)
ISBN 0-8368-6238-4 (softcover)

This North American edition first published in 2006 by
World Almanac® Library
A Member of the WRC Media Family of Companies
330 West Olive Street, Suite 100
Milwaukee, WI 53212 USA

Commissioning editor: Victoria Brooker
Editor: Kelly Davis
Inside design: Chris Halls, www.mindseyedesign.co.uk
Cover design: Hodder Wayland
Series concept and project management by EASI-Educational Resourcing (info@easi-er.co.uk)
Statistical research: Anna Bowden

World Almanac® Library editor: Alan Wachtel
World Almanac® Library cover design: Scott M. Krall

Population Density Map © 2003 UT-Battelle, LLC. All rights reserved.
Data for population density maps reproduced under licence from UT-Battelle, LLC. All rights reserved.
Maps and graphs: Martin Darlison, Encompass Graphics

Picture acknowledgements:
The author and publisher would like to thank the following for allowing their pictures to be reproduced in this publication:
Corbis 9 (Gianni Dagli Orti), 28 (Keith Dannemiller); EASI-Images/Edward Parker 4, 5 and cover, 6, 8, 10, 11, 12, 13, 14, 15, 16, 17, 18, 19, 20, 21, 22, 23, 24, 25, 26, 27, 29, 30, 31, 32, 33, 34, 35, 36, 37, 38, 39, 40, 41, 42, 43 and title page, 44, 45, 46, 47, 48, 49(t), 49(b), 50, 51, 52, 53, 54, 56, 57, 58 and 59.

The directional arrow portrayed on the map on page 7 provides only an approximation of north. The data used to produce the graphics and data panels in this title were the latest available at the time of production.

Printed in China

1 2 3 4 5 6 7 8 9 10 09 08 07 06

CONTENTS

Cover: A Mayan ruin in Yucatán dating from about A.D. 900 overlooks the Caribbean Sea.

Title page: A group of high-school students from Los Mochis strike a pose for the camera.

CHAPTER 1

Mexico – An Overview

Mexico is part of North America, and it is bordered by the wealthy, economically developed United States, to the north, and the economically less developed countries of Central and South America, to the south. It is part of a region known as Latin America, which also includes the countries in Central and South America and the Caribbean that have Spanish or Portuguese as their main language.

The World Bank describes Mexico as a middle-income country. It is more prosperous than most countries of Latin America, but it is less wealthy than the United States. In 2003, the average Mexican's income (before tax) was U.S.$6,230, compared to U.S.$37,610 in the United States and U.S.$2,710 in Brazil. The average income figure, however, hides Mexico's extremes of wealth and poverty. Mexico is one of the most unequal societies in the world.

▼ The second-largest city in the world, Mexico City is sprawling, polluted, and overcrowded. It is the center of government and commerce in Mexico.

MEXICO'S PEOPLE AND HISTORY

The people of Mexico include different cultural groups. The majority are mestizo, or of mixed European and American Indian heritage. The country's population growth rate used to be very high, and about 50 percent of its people today are under twenty-five. Population growth has slowed in recent years, dropping to 1.5 percent a year by 2000. Improvements in health care have extended average life expectancy to seventy-five, compared to only sixty-six in 1980. Three-quarters of the population live in urban areas. In 2005, Mexico City, the capital of Mexico, had the world's second-largest urban population—an estimated 19 million people.

Mexico has a fascinating history that includes the ancient Aztec and Mayan civilizations, colonization by Spain, and a revolution to get rid of a dictator. Mexico's struggle to become an independent, democratic nation has featured charismatic leaders and much bloodshed. The country's dramatic past has helped shape Mexicans' national identity. Mexican culture—which includes ancient rituals, numerous festivals, and a cuisine that combines influences from the distant past and from Spain—is very rich.

 Did You Know?

At 7,350 feet (2,240 meters) above sea level, Mexico City is the fourth-highest city in the world, after La Paz, in Bolivia; Quito, in Ecuador; and Bogotá, in Colombia.

▼ Tulum, in Yucatán, is a Mayan site dating from about A.D. 900. Overlooking the Caribbean, the site was probably a fortress protecting a sea port. Its main temple is visible from the sea.

MOUNTAINS AND MINERALS

Mexico's landscapes range from arid deserts to lush rain forests. Mountains cover about 75 percent of the country's land area. Mexico is one of the most biodiverse countries on Earth, with over 30,000 plant species, almost 450 different mammal species, and over 1,000 types of birds. Located on an active section of Earth's crust, Mexico experiences occasional seismic events, such as earthquakes and volcanic eruptions. Past volcanic activity has left mineral deposits widely distributed across the country. At least sixty minerals were first discovered in Mexico, including silver and copper.

▼ At 18,700 feet (5,700 m), Pico de Orizaba, located in Veracruz, is Mexico's highest mountain. A dormant volcano, it last erupted in 1546. The Aztecs called it Citlatépetl, or "Star Mountain," because moonlight reflects off its snowy peak.

ECONOMIC AND ENVIRONMENTAL CHALLENGES

Mexico faces a number of challenges both in the present day and into the future. One of these is to match economic development with the growing number of people who need jobs. Many Mexican workers migrate to the United States to find work, and some of them do so illegally, which has caused problems between the governments of Mexico and the United States. Since the 1994 North American Free Trade Agreement (NAFTA), the number of factories that manufacture goods for sale in the United States, known as maquiladoras, built just south of the border into Mexico has increased. These provide the largely unskilled jobs for which many Mexicans are looking. Many of these factories, however, produce hazardous waste that causes serious environmental problems. Future economic development in the country needs to be carried out in ways that do not harm the environment. In the past, industrialization in Mexico has caused a great deal of environmental damage. Mexico's government now recognizes an urgent need to repair this damage and to ensure that conservation is given high priority.

Physical Geography Data

- Land area: 742,486 sq miles/1,923,040 sq km
- Water area: 19,116 sq miles/49,510 sq km
- Total area: 761,602 sq miles/1,972,550 sq km
- World rank (by area): 15
- Land boundaries: 2,703 miles/4,350 km
- Border countries: Belize, Guatemala, U.S.
- Coastline: 5,797 miles/9,330 km
- Highest point: Pico de Orizaba (18,700 feet/5,700 m)
- Lowest point: Laguna Salada (-33 ft/-10 m)

Source: CIA World Factbook

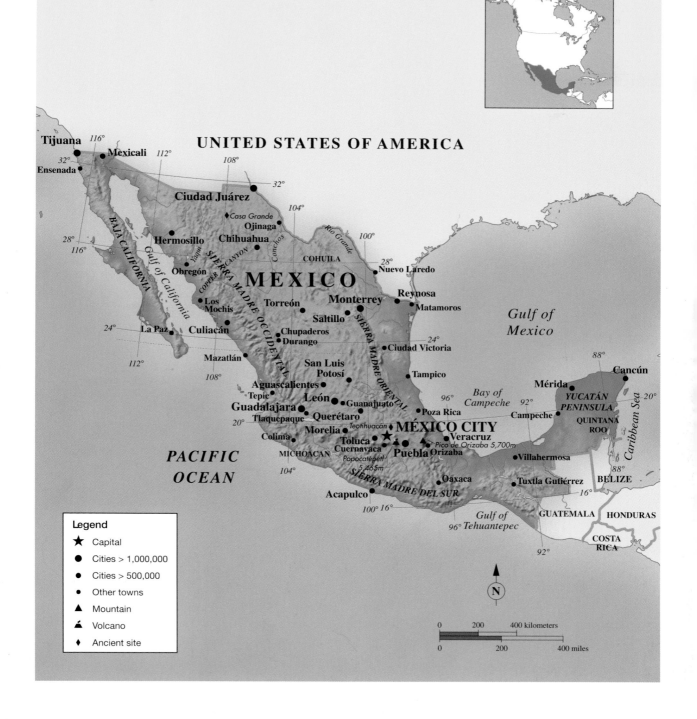

UNITED STATES OF AMERICA

Tijuana
Mexicali
Ensenada
Ciudad Juárez
♦Casa Grande
Ojinaga
Hermosillo
Chihuahua
Obregón
COHUILA
Rio Grande
Nuevo Laredo
MEXICO
Reynosa
Los Mochis
Torreón
Monterrey
Matamoros
Saltillo
Chupaderos
Durango
Ciudad Victoria
La Paz
Culiacán
Mazatlán
San Luis Potosí
Tampico
BAJA CALIFORNIA
Gulf of California
SIERRA MADRE OCCIDENTAL
COPPER CANYON
Yaqui
Conchos
SIERRA MADRE ORIENTAL

Gulf of Mexico

Mérida
Cancún
YUCATÁN PENINSULA
QUINTANA ROO
Campeche
Caribbean Sea

Aguascalientes
Tepic
León
Guanajuato
Bay of Campeche
Guadalajara
Tlaquepaque
Querétaro
Poza Rica
Morelia
Teotihuacán
MÉXICO CITY
Colima
Toluca
Veracruz
Cuernavaca
Popocatépetl 5,465m
Puebla Orizaba
Pico de Orizaba 5,700m
MICHOACAN
Villahermosa

PACIFIC OCEAN

SIERRA MADRE DEL SUR
Oaxaca
Tuxtla Gutiérrez
BELIZE
Acapulco
Gulf of Tehuantepec
GUATEMALA   HONDURAS
COSTA RICA

116° 112° 108° 104° 100° 32° 28° 24° 20° 16° 96° 92° 88°

N

Legend
★ Capital
● Cities > 1,000,000
● Cities > 500,000
• Other towns
▲ Mountain
◮ Volcano
♦ Ancient site

0   200   400 kilometers
0   200   400 miles

CHAPTER 2

History

Ancient Mexico was part of a region called Mesoamerica. Bigger than present-day Mexico, Mesoamerica included areas to the north that today make up Texas, New Mexico, Arizona, and California and areas to the south that are now Belize, Guatemala, El Salvador, Honduras, and Nicaragua.

▼ This pyramid rises to over 197 feet (60 meters). It is among the biggest pyramids in the world, and it dominates the archaeological site of Teotihuacán. Covering an area of 8 square miles (20 square kilometers),Teotihuacán was one of the largest cities of the ancient world.

ANCIENT CIVILIZATIONS

Between about 1500 B.C. and A.D. 1300, many civilizations lived in the area that eventually became modern-day Mexico. The first of these were the Olmec. Around 500 B.C., as the Olmec died out, other civilizations were growing. From about 200 B.C. to A.D. 900, many cities were established, including Teotihuacán, near present-day Mexico City. Between A.D. 400 and 500, Teotihuacán was the sixth-largest city in the world, with a population of over 150,000. During the seventh century, however, the city outgrew its water and food resources and declined. Another important civilization at this time was the Maya. The Maya are thought to have lived in an area encompassing El Salvador, Guatemala, and southern Mexico. They built cities and religious sites and had sophisticated systems of writing, mathematics, and

▲ The Aztec grew crops on *chinampas*, which are raised floating beds made from reeds, mud, and manure.

astronomy. In mathematics, for example, they used a base-twenty counting system. In astronomy, they observed and predicted solar and lunar eclipses.

The last great Mesoamerican civilization was the Aztec. The Aztecs had a well-developed system of agriculture and an efficient military force. Led by their ruler, Tlacaelel, they expanded their territory, and by the late 1400s, they were the most powerful people in the area that is present-day Mexico.

THE SPANISH CONQUEST

In 1519, Hernán Cortés, a Spanish explorer, led Spanish troops known as *los conquistadores* (meaning "the conquerors") to Mexico in search of gold and silver. They landed at Veracruz and headed for Tenochtitlán.

Focus on: Tenochtitlán

The Aztecs originally migrated from the north into central Mexico. They believed that one of their gods, Huitzilopochtli, prophesied that they would settle where an eagle was seen sitting on a cactus eating a snake. The eagle was apparently sighted on an island in Lake Texcoco and the city of Tenochtitlán was founded. Tenochtitlán flourished, and the Aztecs fought many wars to gain territory and to capture people for sacrifice to their gods who, they believed, needed human hearts in return for good harvests. Mexico City is located on the former site of Tenochtitlán.

The king of the Aztecs, Montezuma II, at first thought that Cortés was the great god Huitzilopochtli returning and greeted him warmly. The Spanish, however, murdered the Aztec king and took over Tenochtitlán. By 1521, the Aztecs had been defeated, and Mexico had been named New Spain. Three centuries of Spanish colonial rule followed, and Spain amassed great wealth from Mexico's resources, including its rich silver deposits. In New Spain, wealthy Spanish colonists ruled over the powerless indigenous population.

THE FIGHT FOR INDEPENDENCE AND BEYOND

Poor peasants in the rural areas deeply resented the inequalities of colonial society. The fight for independence from Spain began in 1810, led by Miguel Hidalgo, a priest. Hidalgo was executed, but the unrest continued. After many uprisings and approximately 600,000 deaths, Mexico finally won its independence in 1821. Every year on September 16, Mexicans still celebrate the day when Hidalgo called them to rise up and fight for their freedom.

From the 1820s to the 1850s, many changes of government took place in Mexico. General Antonio Lopez de Santa Ana took over the presidency eleven times between 1823 and 1855. Under his leadership, Mexico lost nearly half its territory to the United States in a war that lasted from 1846 to 1848. Santa Ana was overthrown soon after this. Civil war and an invasion by France followed, before another army officer, Porfirio Diaz, became president in 1876. Diaz ruled as a ruthless dictator for thirty-four years.

◀ The Angel of Independence monument, erected in Mexico City in 1910, commemorates those who fought against Spanish colonial rule.

THE MEXICAN REVOLUTION

The Mexican Revolution began in 1910 when Porfirio Diaz declared himself president again and forced his opponent, Francisco Madero, to flee to Texas. Opposition to Diaz was widespread. The middle classes wanted more political power, most peasants had no land, and living conditions in urban areas were terrible. In Mexico City, for example, health care, water, and sanitation facilities were so poor that average life expectancy was only twenty-four years. Peasants' and workers' uprisings, led by Emiliano Zapata, Venustiano Carranza, and Pancho Villa, forced Diaz to resign in 1911.

Francisco Madero then became president, but the unrest continued, and he too resigned. He was replaced by the ruthless and unpopular General Victoriano Huerta. The revolutionary leaders Zapata, Carranza, and Villa joined forces again to oppose Huerta. After two more years of fighting and the withdrawal of U.S.-government support for Huerta, the revolutionaries

▲ On Independence Day, fiestas and parades, with fireworks, music, and children dressed in traditional clothing, take place throughout Mexico.

Focus on: Porfirio Diaz

After a military coup, Porfirio Diaz proclaimed himself president. Diaz introduced a program of modernization, and Mexico's economy thrived, but he used his brutal police force to suppress any opposition to his rule. He also gave land to his trusted supporters while most Mexicans remained poor and landless.

 Did You Know?

In 1521, Mexico's indigenous population was estimated at twenty million. By the mid-seventeenth century, it had dropped to one million. The main reason for this high death rate was diseases, such as smallpox and measles, that were brought into Mexico by Europeans.

succeeded, and Huerta fled. The revolutionary leaders then came to power, but they could not agree which of them should be in charge. Zapata and Villa together opposed Carranza and marched into Mexico City to take over the National Palace. However, both Zapata, who came from the southern state of Morelos, and Villa, from the northern city of Chihuahua, were more concerned with their home regions and soon returned to them.

Carranza's army defeated Villa's forces, and Carranza became president in 1917, establishing the constitution that is still in place in the country today. Carranza, however, did not carry out all his promises, and fighting continued between his forces and Zapata's supporters. Zapata was assassinated in 1919, and Carranza was assassinated the following year. By 1923, Villa had also been assassinated. Altogether, between one and two million people either were killed or had fled the country during the Mexican Revolution.

▼ This detail from Diego Rivera's mural that depicts the history of Mexico shows leaders of the Mexican Revolution, including Emiliano Zapata, who is pictured behind the banner at the back.

FROM REVOLUTION TO THE TWENTY-FIRST CENTURY

Between 1934 and 1940, oil nationalization, land reform, and industrial expansion benefited many Mexicans. Later, between 1946 and 1970, industrial production grew steadily. During the 1960s, however, Mexican oil reserves began to run out, oil was imported, and prices rose. Economic and political problems led to anti-government protests, which were often brutally suppressed. In 1968, hundreds were killed or injured when security forces fired on a demonstration in Mexico City. Further economic and political crises occurred in the 1980s and 1990s, including a 1994 uprising of indigenous people in Chiapas who were protesting against inequality.

For just over seventy years, beginning in 1929, Mexico was controlled by the PRI, or the Partido Revolucionario Institucional (the Institutional Revolutionary Party). The PRI had originally been formed to unite the victors of the Revolution. At first, it had popular support, but from the 1970s on, evidence showed that bribery and fraud were being used to keep the party in power. The PRI's dominance ended in 2000 when the opposition party won the presidential election. The PRI, however, remained dominant in Mexico's congress.

Focus on: The Haciendas

During Porfirio Diaz's rule, large country estates called haciendas were owned by a few wealthy people. The haciendas were huge—one of them, in the northern state of Chihuahua, was as big as Belgium—and the landowners grew cash crops such as coffee or sisal. Local people provided the labor, working long, hard hours. In 1910, the revolutionary leader Emiliano Zapata demanded that the haciendas be divided up and given to the peasants. Most of the estates were eventually broken up, although some wealthy landowners managed to retain control of their property.

▶ The Castle of Chapultepec, in Mexico City, was the home of Maximilian, who was emperor of Mexico from 1864 to 1867, and Lázaro Cárdenas, who was Mexico's president from 1934 to 1940.

CHAPTER 3

Landscape and Climate

Mexico covers an area of 742,486 sq miles (1,923,040 sq km). It is third in size, after Argentina and Brazil, in Latin America, and it is about four times the size of France. It shares borders with the United States, to the north, and with Belize and Guatemala, to the south. To the west is the Pacific Ocean, and to the east is the Gulf of Mexico (part of the Caribbean). Within this large country, varied physical landscapes and climates—including desert, tropical rain forest, and temperate forest—provide different habitats for flora and fauna.

MOUNTAINS AND BEACHES

Two of Mexico's most striking landscape features are its great mountain ranges, the Sierra Madre Occidental and the Sierra Madre Oriental. These ranges both run north to south, parallel with the Pacific and Gulf coasts. Between the two Sierra mountain ranges is the Central Plateau. The southern section of the Central Plateau contains valleys originally formed by ancient lakes about thirty-nine thousand years ago. One of these, the Valley of Mexico, is home to 20 percent of Mexico's population. The country has low-lying coastal areas in the south, with sandy beaches, rocky headlands and islets, mangrove swamps, and even an offshore coral reef at Quintana Roo. Mexico's coastline is 5,797 miles (9,330 kilometers) in length—much longer than the coastline of any other Latin American country.

◀ Playa del Carmen, at Quintana Roo, is typical of the fine white-sand beaches found along the Caribbean coastline of the Yucatán Peninsula. Just offshore is the world's second-longest coral reef. The beaches, the reef, and the warm waters in this area attract a variety of sea life, including dolphins and turtles.

WHERE THE PLATES OF EARTH'S CRUST MEET

Mexico is on the edge of one of the most dynamic tectonic areas in the world. The Pacific Ocean is surrounded by the boundaries at which the plates that make up Earth's crust meet. Along these boundaries are many of the world's volcanoes, which is why this area is known as the Pacific Ring of Fire. One of the boundaries runs down the Pacific coast of Mexico, with Baja California lying along the famous San Andreas Fault. Further north, this fault runs through San Francisco. In the past, volcanoes, earthquakes, and tsunamis have all occurred in Mexico. The most serious earthquake in recent times, which measured 8.1 on the Richter scale, caused devastation in Mexico City in 1985. More than twenty thousand people were killed, many of them living in inner-city, multistory apartment buildings that collapsed during the earthquake.

▲ At 17,930 feet (5,465 m), the volcano Popocatépetl is Mexico's second-highest peak.

 Did You Know?

The Copper Canyon, in the Sierra Madre Occidental, is deeper than the Grand Canyon.

Focus on: Volcano Popocatépetl

On a clear day, the volcano Popocatépetl and its neighboring peak, Iztaccihuatl, can be seen from Mexico City. These are two of Mexico's highest peaks, and they are often capped with snow. In December 2000, "Popo," as the volcano is known to locals, erupted for the first time since the 1920s. The relatively small eruption did not kill anyone, but fifty-six million people were evacuated from the area. A major eruption could threaten thirty million people.

INFLUENCES ON THE CLIMATE

Mexico has a number of different climatic zones that vary according to latitude, altitude, and proximity to the sea. Half of Mexico lies south of the Tropic of Cancer, and this region tends to be hot and humid. In the north of the country, temperatures are also high, but the climate tends to be much drier, mainly because the prevailing winds have already lost their moisture before they reach northern Mexico. Near the coasts, the influence of the sea can be felt. The cold Californian sea current, for example, lowers temperatures and rainfall on Mexico's Pacific coast. Meanwhile, on the Gulf of Mexico coast, warm waters create a tropical climate. Inland,

higher-altitude, mountainous areas tend to have lower temperatures and increased rainfall. Apart from a rainy season, which moves from south to north from May to October, the climate in this area does not vary much.

EFFECTS OF THE CLIMATE ON PEOPLE AND VEGETATION

Between June and November, parts of the Gulf of Mexico coast are likely to be affected by hurricanes that move in from the Caribbean. Hurricanes also occur, but less frequently, along the Pacific coast. Hurricane winds can lead to loss of life and cause considerable damage to property. The heavy rains hurricanes bring may cause mudslides and flooding on the mountainsides. Rainfall in the highland areas, however, replenishes reservoirs that provide much-needed water for urban areas and agriculture. The country's generally high temperatures also help to attract tourists.

Mexico's variety of climates is reflected in the many different types of vegetation found throughout the country. In the arid region of the north, only drought-resistant plants such as cacti can survive. The more temperate and humid zones have more than twenty thousand species of flowering plants. At the higher altitudes inland, there are mixed forests that include Montezuma pines, oaks, and cypresses. To the south, toward the coast of the Gulf of Mexico, are the last remaining areas of tropical rain forest in Mexico.

◀ Over half of Mexico is classified as arid, which means that it receives less than 4 inches (10 centimeters) of rainfall per year. Cacti, such as this one grown on Tiburon Island in the Gulf of California, have adapted to the dry conditions.

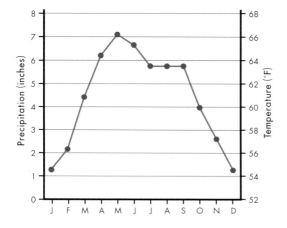

▲ Many of Mexico's rain forest areas have been cleared for farming. Located in Oaxaca, this is one of the country's few remaining rain forests.

▲ Average monthly climate conditions in Mexico City

 Did You Know?

About 75 percent of Mexico is mountainous. Much of the country's high terrain is over 3,280 feet (1,000 m) above sea level. The country's highest peak is Pico de Orizaba, at 18,700 feet (5,700 m).

 Did You Know?

Temperatures below freezing are not unusual at altitudes above 9,842 feet (3,000 m) in the Mexican part of the Sierra mountain ranges. The loftiest peaks have permanent snow. Mexico's highest temperatures are experienced in the northern area. In the desert regions of the northeast, the average July temperature is 95 °F (35 °C). A maximum of 117 °F (47 °C) has been recorded at Guaymas, in the northwest.

CHAPTER 4

Population and Settlements

Mexico has a total population of about 102.5 million. The country's population has increased from 12 million in 1900, with its most rapid growth—at the rate of 3.5 percent a year—in the 1960s. It is still growing but at a slower rate of about 1.5 percent each year, which is still relatively high. Life expectancy in Mexico has generally increased, with a noticeable drop in infant mortality because of improved health care. As a result of these trends, people under twenty-five make up half the country's population. Some groups in Mexican society—mostly indigenous peoples—still have high death and infant mortality rates because of poverty and poor living conditions.

A DIVERSE PEOPLE

Mexico's population is very diverse. It has the largest number of different indigenous peoples of any Latin American country. These peoples, who are descendants of Mexico's ancient civilizations, such as the Maya, include many different groups. Approximately sixty indigenous languages are still spoken in the country. The majority of Mexicans are mestizo, or of mixed indigenous and Spanish heritage.

▼ A Mexican family with young children sits down to a meal at home. Compared to many countries that are more economically developed, Mexico has a young population.

MOVEMENT INTO AND OUT OF MEXICO

People migrate into Mexico in the south from the relatively poor countries of Guatemala and El Salvador, many entering illegally. Some stay in Mexico, but for many, their goal is to travel north through Mexico and into the United States. Crossing this southern border into

▲ The Maya, one of Mexico's many indigenous groups, live in the Yucatán region.

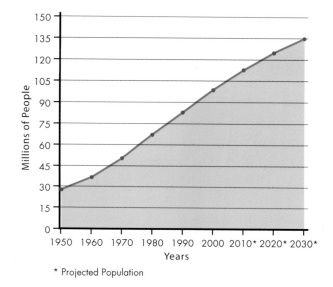

* Projected Population

▲ Population growth, 1950–2030

Population Data

- Population: 104.9 million
- Population 0–14 yrs: 32%
- Population 15–64 yrs: 63%
- Population 65+ yrs: 5%
- Population growth rate (2000–2005): 1.5%
- Population density: 141.3 per sq mile/ 54.5 per sq km
- Urban population: 76%
- Major cities: Mexico City 19,013,000; Guadalajara 3,905,000; Monterrey 3,517,000

Sources: United Nations and World Bank

Mexico illegally is incredibly risky. Attempts to jump onto moving freight trains under cover of darkness often result in injury or death. The chances of being caught by Mexico's police are also high, with over 150,000 people being detained and sent back each year. In Mexico's north, large numbers of people immigrate—both legally and illegally—over the country's border with the United States.

MOVEMENT WITHIN MEXICO

Mexico's population is unevenly distributed. About 20 percent of its people live in the Valley of Mexico, which is an area of only 127 sq miles (330 sq km). Since the 1980s, many people have moved to the industrial towns of northern Mexico in search of jobs. These towns are on or near Mexico's border with the United States and are home to thousands of maquiladoras, or factories in which goods are manufactured for sale in the United States. Many Mexicans are eager to work in these factories because the wage rates are higher than elsewhere in the country. Northern towns, such as Tijuana and Ciudad Juárez, are now among the fastest-growing settlements in Mexico.

Over the past fifty years, increasing migration from the countryside has led to the numbers living in towns and cities almost doubling. Today, more than 75 percent of Mexico's population lives in urban areas. Many people

◀ The majority of Mexicans live in overcrowded industrial towns like Guanajuato (shown here).

Focus on: Illegal Immigration into the United States

Because U.S. immigration officials patrol much of the border of Mexico and the United States, illegal migrants aim to cross the border where they are unlikely to be detected. Many used to struggle across the Rio Bravo/Rio Grande River, which led to them being called "wetbacks" as an insult. Since 1994, however, when Operation Gatekeeper was introduced by President Bill Clinton, the river has been more tightly patrolled. Many migrants now try to enter the United States through the sparsely populated desert of Arizona.

About five hundred illegal migrants are thought to die each year from thirst and heat exhaustion. Those who do survive are still likely to be arrested, with over one million Mexicans detained yearly in the United States before being sent back to Mexico. Illegal migrants, many of whom are from the poorest groups in Mexico, are likely to keep trying to enter the United States because they believe that living in the United States will give them access to educational opportunities, well-paid jobs, and good health care.

move to Mexico City because it is both the country's capital and its largest city. Mexico City is about five times bigger than Guadalajara, the next-largest city in Mexico.

Mexico City attracts people because they believe the city has more job opportunities and a better quality of life. When they get there, however, the reality may be quite different. The lack of adequate housing in Mexico City means that many people end up living in shantytowns without clean water or sanitation facilities. The same problems often face people moving to cities such as Guadalajara and the northern industrial towns, in which conditions are often very poor, with too few facilities for the size of the population living there.

Many small farmers are leaving rural areas because soil erosion has left them with no good land to farm. In addition, problems exist with land ownership. Although one of the main aims of the Mexican Revolution was to give everyone equal access to land, much of the country's land is still concentrated in the hands of a few rich landowners. In the years immediately following the Mexican Revolution, many of the large estates were split up and smaller parcels of land were given to landless peasants in the local communities. Over the years, these parcels of land have been divided up to be passed to the children of farmers. Today, 60 percent of them are 5 acres (2 hectares) or less in size, which is too little to provide a living.

 Did You Know?

The population of Mexico City has grown from 16,790,000 in 1995 to 19,013,000 in 2005. This growth is the equivalent of adding 609 people every day over the 10-year period.

▼ Rural Mexico has many small, scattered settlements, such as this one in the desert state of Cohuila.

CHAPTER 5

Government and Politics

Mexico is a federal republic made up of thirty-one states and the federal district of Mexico City. The country's president is both head of the government and head of state, the official who represents Mexico in the international community. Mexico is governed by the National Congress, which is made up of the Senate (with 128 senators) and the Federal Chamber of Deputies (with 500 deputies). The senators and deputies, who are democratically elected by citizens over eighteen years old, represent the states that make up the federal republic. Presidential elections are held every six years, and an individual president can serve only one term.

DEMOCRACY AND CORRUPTION

In name, Mexico has been a democracy since the establishment of the Mexican federal republic in 1824. From 1929 until 2000, however, the country was effectively a one-party state. The Partido Revolucionario Institucional (PRI), originally formed in 1929, won all elections. Until the 1970s, the PRI won as a result of popularity. Later, when voters became disillusioned by the country's economic problems, it won by suppressing official opposition, and corruption was widespread. Not surprisingly, the defeat of the PRI's presidential candidate in 2000 was seen as a major turning point in Mexico's history. Since then, the new government, headed by Vicente Fox of the National Action Party, has been trying to tackle the problems of corruption and political repression. The National Congress has gained more power to balance that of the president.

◀ A giant Mexican flag flies in the Zócalo, Mexico City's main square. After the political turbulence of the past, Mexicans are now enjoying a reasonably stable period in their country's history.

Mexico's Constitution, which lays down the rights and duties of Mexican citizens, dates from 1917 and was drawn up to meet the demands of the Revolution for freedom and equal rights. Although equality is still held to be important, certain groups in Mexican society still wield more power than others.

Many indigenous peoples in Mexico feel their rights are not recognized, and this feeling led to antigovernment protests in Chiapas in 1994. Also, women hold only 5 percent of the decision-making jobs in Mexico's government. In spite of official commitment to improving this situation, progress has been slow.

Focus on: Indian Uprising in Chiapas

In 1994, the Ejército Zapatista de Liberación Nacional (Zapatista National Liberation Army, or EZLN) led armed uprisings of the Indian people in the state of Chiapas, in southern Mexico, calling for greater recognition of Indians' rights. The indigenous people of this area were among the poorest in Mexico. They feared that Mexico's signing of the North American Free Trade Agreement (NAFTA) was going to make them poorer by attracting even more business to the north of Mexico, which is closer to the United States. They were also concerned that NAFTA would lead to cheap U.S. agricultural goods competing with those produced by farmers in the Chiapas region. Following fighting between the EZLN and government troops, a cease-fire was called, and it remains in place. In 2001, new laws were passed giving indigenous people more rights. Because, however, the EZLN does not believe that these laws went far enough in promoting Indian rights, they have continued their political campaign nonviolently.

▼ People fish near a border-patrol post at Ojinaga. This post is one of many such posts set up on the U.S. side of the Rio Bravo (or Rio Grande, as it is called in the United States) to combat the problem of Mexican migrants trying to enter the United States illegally.

MEXICO'S RELATIONSHIP WITH THE UNITED STATES

Mexico and the United States have strong economic links. In 1994, they both signed, along with Canada, the North American Free Trade Agreement (NAFTA). NAFTA promotes trade between its member countries and has eased the movement of goods and money between them. Mexico and the United States also agree on many foreign policy issues. For example, the two governments work closely in trying to stop drug trafficking across their border. They take very different approaches, however, to the problem of illegal migration from Mexico to the United States. Mexico's government favors the introduction of temporary visas that would allow Mexicans to move to the United States for short periods and cross back to visit their families, while the United States is more inclined to tighten up border controls because of worries about a huge influx of poor people from Mexico.

▼ People wait in their cars at a U.S. inspection station at Tijuana. Tijuana is one of the world's busiest border-crossing points.

The governments of Mexico and the United States also cooperate in tackling environmental issues that affect both sides of the border. Several decision-making bodies, such as the International Boundary and Water Commission and the Border Environment Cooperation Commission (BECC), have equal numbers of Mexican and American delegates. Through these bodies, joint projects have been undertaken on problems related to the protection of shared habitats, such as the deserts of Sonora/Arizona; water supply; waste disposal; and air quality.

 Did You Know?

In 1967, Mexican president Gustavo Diaz Ordaz initiated the drafting of a treaty prohibiting Latin American and Caribbean countries from acquiring nuclear weapons. The Treaty of Tlatelolco, which is named after the district in Mexico City where it was drafted, has now been signed by all thirty-three Latin American and Caribbean countries.

A MEMBER OF THE INTERNATIONAL COMMUNITY

Mexico has diplomatic relations with over 170 countries and is a member of several international organizations. Mexico was one of the first countries to join the United Nations (UN) when the UN was formed in 1945. In 1994, Mexico also became the first Latin American country to join the Organization for Economic Cooperation and Development (OECD), set up in 1961. Mexico has trade agreements with other Latin American countries, including Guatemala, El Salvador, and Honduras, and the European Union (EU), in an attempt to balance its dependence on the United States, which buys almost 90 percent of the country's exports. Mexico was also a founding member of the World Trade Organization (WTO), established in 1995.

▼ The port of Veracruz plays a vital role in Mexico's import and export trade, handling many different types of cargo, including textiles, iron, steel, and chemicals.

CHAPTER 6

Energy and Resources

Mexico is the fifth-largest producer of oil in the world. It is not, however, a member of the Organization of Petroleum Exporting Countries (OPEC). Major oil reserves were first found in the country in the 1880s, but they began to run dry, and by 1971, Mexico was importing oil. Big new reserves were discovered in the mid-1970s, and these have continued to provide Mexico with oil, both for its own needs and for export to other countries. Because oil is a major source of income for Mexico and the state oil company, PEMEX, provides about one-third of the government's revenue, world oil prices directly affect Mexico's economy. During the 1970s, oil accounted for 78 percent of all Mexican exports. In 1981, when oil prices dropped, Mexico's income fell sharply, and it was unable to pay back money it had borrowed from foreign investors. Since then, Mexico has tried to balance its economy by developing its manufacturing and tourism industries.

GAS RESERVES

Mexico also produces natural gas, mainly in the south of the country. Until recently, it has not been used to meet the country's energy needs. Mexico's government now wants to develop the use of natural gas because it is a cleaner fuel than oil, and it aims to double natural gas use by 2010. Increased use of natural gas will require more refineries and more pipelines to transport the gas from the country's south to its north, where industrial demand for energy is higher. Until these pipelines and refineries can be built, Mexico continues to import natural gas from the United States.

◀ PEMEX, Mexico's state-owned oil company, was established in 1938. It owns all the country's gas stations.

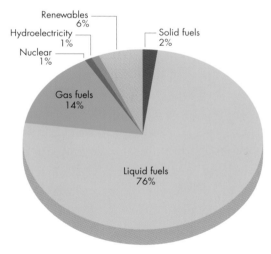

▲ Gas being flared off at an oil refinery in Tampico. Gas vapors are a by-product of oil drilling, and they are flared in order to dispose of them.

ELECTRICITY GENERATION

About 92 percent of Mexico's electricity is generated from oil, gas, and coal. Of the remainder, 1 percent is from hydroelectric power (HEP), 1 percent from nuclear power plants, and 6 percent from renewable sources. With continued industrial development, a growing population, and increasing use of electricity in homes, Mexico's electricity consumption is steadily increasing. Demand may very soon outstrip supply.

Mexico has plans to produce more electricity, including developing renewable sources. HEP has been an important electricity source in the past but droughts in northern Mexico have caused serious problems with its use. Other sources to be expanded are geothermal, solar, and wind power. The government now seems

▲ Energy use by type

 Did You Know?

Mexico has a great deal of potential for generating electricity from geothermal energy, which is derived from natural heat in Earth's crust. At present, the country uses about 955 megawatts of electricity generated from geothermal energy, but it has been estimated that this could be expanded to 8,000 megawatts.

to be recognizing the advantages of these renewable forms of energy. Wind power plants are being set up in Oaxaca.

Energy Data

📁 Energy consumption as % of world total: 1.4%

📁 Energy consumption by sector (% of total):
Industry: 41
Transportation: 38
Agriculture: 2
Services: 3
Residential: 16

📁 CO_2 emissions as % of world total: 1.5

📁 CO_2 emissions per capita in tons per year: 4.1

Source: World Resources Institute

MINERALS AND METALS

Largely because of the intense seismic activity that affects its region, Mexico is very rich in minerals, including silver, gold, copper, lead, tungsten, iron ore, and zinc. However, only about 5 percent of the country's mineral reserves have been exploited. This is partly because of lack of investment and partly because of the difficulty of extracting mineral deposits from mountainous terrain.

Mexico is the world's largest producer of silver. The country produces about 14 percent of the world's silver each year, and silver production provides about 2 percent of Mexico's gross domestic product (GDP). Until its closure in 1998, the world's largest silver mine was at Real de Angeles. This mine produced about 11,000

▶ Gold has been mined in Mexico for centuries. In this picture, a miner drills for gold in a mine tunnel in the state of Durango, in central Mexico.

tons (10,000 metric tons) of ore a day, from which about 243 tons (220 metric tons) of silver could be extracted. Silver production continues at other mines, including Fresnillo, in Zacatecas. Much of Mexico's silver output is exported, mainly to the United States, although some is retained for Mexican use.

OTHER RICHES FROM THE LAND AND SEA

Timber—including softwoods, such as pine, and hardwoods, such as mahogany—is an important resource for Mexico. Large-scale commercial forestry, however, has led to extensive areas in the country becoming deforested, with 311,615 acres (770,000 ha) per year having been cleared between 1993 and 2000. This problem is beginning to be addressed with replanting

programs and an emphasis on more sustainable use. Fishing also provides a valuable source of income for inhabitants of some coastal and lakeside settlements. The main catches from the Pacific include lobsters, sardines, and anchovies, while the Gulf of Mexico and the Caribbean provide shrimp, snape, mackerel, and mullet.

The commercial potential of Mexico's diverse landscapes and wildlife is increasingly being recognized, with major developments in eco-tourism and adventure tourism. With more than 30,000 plant species, including cacti and orchids; almost 450 different mammals, such as elephant seals, Mexican bighorn sheep, and black bears; and over 100,000 species of birds, including hummingbirds, eagles, and pelicans, Mexico has much to appeal to anyone with an interest in nature. Mexico's varied natural environments also offer opportunities for outdoor activities such as climbing, hiking, and white-water rafting.

▼ Mexico's indigenous people have always fished the seas around the Baja California coastline.

Focus on: Community Forestry Project

With the help of the Community Forestry Project, which is funded by the World Bank, small communities in Mexico are being helped to conserve their forest resources and protect endangered species. Over five hundred indigenous communities have received money and technical assistance to help them develop sources of income that are sustainable. Some groups have set up shade-grown coffee cooperatives that preserve the forest canopy created by valuable tropical trees, rather than felling the valuable trees for timber.

CHAPTER 7

Economy and Income

Mexico is now considered by the World Bank to be a middle-economy country, meaning that its gross national income (GNI) is higher than that of less developed countries but lower than that of fully industrialized ones, such as the United States and Britain. The development of a range of industries, including car and electronics manufacturing, has helped Mexico become one of the strongest economies in Latin America. Guadalajara, the capital of the central state of Jalisco, which is known as Mexico's "Silicon Valley," is a center for the production of high-tech electronic goods and has helped to make Mexico one of the world leaders in this field.

Tourism has become a major source of employment in Mexico and the country's third most important source of foreign income, following oil and remittances, or money sent back to Mexico by Mexicans working in other countries. In terms of the number of people they employ, Mexico's manufacturing and service industries have developed in recent years, while its agricultural industry has shrunk. All of Mexico's industries contribute to its economy by earning money from exports.

FREE TRADE WITH THE U.S.

In 1994, Mexico signed the North American Free Trade Agreement (NAFTA) with the United States and Canada, with the aim of eliminating all trade tariffs by 2010. Since then, trade between the three countries has tripled. In many ways, Mexico has benefited from NAFTA. For example, its economy grew by over 5 percent per year in 1999 and 2000. Mexico is now the United States's second-largest trading partner (Canada is

◀ With its sandy beaches and luxurious hotels, Cancún, located on the Yucatán Peninsula, is popular with both wealthy Mexicans and foreign tourists.

the largest), with 88 percent of its exports going to the United States. This close relationship has obviously stimulated certain sectors of Mexico's economy, such as the manufacturing of electronic goods and the production of crops such as

Economic Data

- 📁 Gross National Income (GNI) in U.S.$: 637,159,200,000
- 📁 World rank by GNI: 10
- 📁 GNI per capita in U.S.$: 6,230
- 📁 World rank by GNI per capita: 68
- 📁 Economic growth: 1%

Source: World Bank

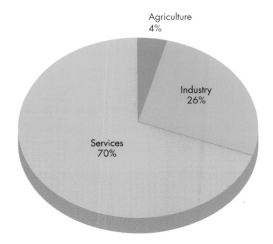

Agriculture
4%

Industry
26%

Services
70%

▲ Contribution by sector to national income

 Did You Know?

Mexico now produces 98 percent of the televisions sold in North America.

▶ Maize is Mexico's main agricultural product, and it is a staple food of its people's diet. It is grown both on a large-scale commercial basis and by subsistence farmers.

tomatoes. Being so strongly linked to the U.S. economy, however, does have its problems. This was demonstrated in 2001 when an economic downturn in the United States resulted in no growth in the Mexican economy. The economic benefits of trading with the United States have also been largely concentrated in northern and central Mexico, with the south left behind.

WOMEN IN THE WORKFORCE

Women made up 37 percent of Mexico's workforce in 2002. This percentage has more than doubled over twenty years, partly because of new attitudes introduced by the feminist movement, which encouraged women to become economically independent. Another reason for its increase in female workers was the economic hardship that Mexico experienced

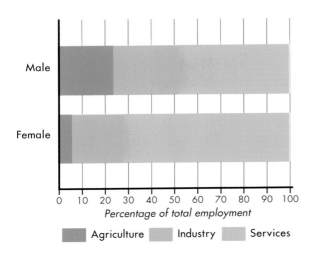

▲ Labor force by sector and gender

INEQUALITY AND POVERTY

Mexico has one of the most unequal distributions of wealth in the world, with 20 percent of the population owning 55 percent of the wealth. In 2000, twenty-three million Mexicans were living in extreme poverty, at times unable to afford even essential food. Poverty is mainly concentrated in the rural south, where there are fewer industries and smaller farms. Poverty is also a problem for small-scale farmers in the north who depend on irrigation systems because they cannot afford to run these systems efficiently, as well as for many residents of the rapidly growing cities in the north and south.

during the 1980s, which required that women, as well as men, needed to earn money to make ends meet. Since the 1980s, more married women in Mexico have been working instead of devoting themselves to homemaking and children. In Mexico, however, women still are paid less than men. For example, in the country's manufacturing industries, women's wages are 30 percent lower than men's wages.

These economic problems are not easy to solve. Many poor Mexicans leave their homes to migrate to the United States, in the hope of improving their income and quality of life. Once in the United States, they often find jobs,

▼ Poor farmers in Mexico's rural areas still use donkeys as their main means of transportation. This farmer is in the state of Veracruz.

although the jobs they find generally do not pay well. Much of their income is sent back to their families in Mexico, and this money is one of the biggest sources of foreign income for Mexico. The government is trying to deal with rural poverty. In association with the World Bank, it has drawn up the Development Strategy for the Mexican Southern States, a program to help the region that is home to 25 percent of all Mexicans living in extreme poverty.

Focus on: Quality of Life in the Border Region

▲ Four maquiladora workers in Tijuana take a lunch break before returning for their afternoon shift.

Mexico's northern region, which runs along its 1,958 mile (3,153 km) border with the United States, is the most rapidly developing area in the country. It has the highest rates of industrial growth and employment. Over the past twenty years, more than three thousand factories have been built along the U.S.-Mexico border. Known as maquiladoras, these factories manufacture goods for the U.S. market. Many are owned by foreign companies that exploit the low wage rates of Mexican workers in order to increase their profits. These wages may be low by U.S. standards, but they are relatively high compared to wages elsewhere in Mexico. These factory jobs also offer permanent, regular income and, thus, have helped to strengthen the northern region's economy. Development in Mexico's northern region also has disadvantages. Increases in the number of factories and the number of trucks transporting goods across the border have led to very high levels of air pollution. Although cooperation between Mexico and the United States has succeeded in tackling some environmental issues in this region, problems with household waste disposal and water supplies still endanger the health of the local population.

CHAPTER 8

Global Connections

Mexico has trade links with many countries. Its major trading commitment is the North American Free Trade Agreement (NAFTA), in which it participates with the United States and Canada. The country also has free trade agreements with the European Union (EU) and with other Latin American countries.

Mexico was a founding member of the World Trade Organization (WTO), and it is also a member of the Organization for Economic Cooperation and Development (OECD) and the Asia-Pacific Economic Cooperation forum (APEC). Each of these organizations offers opportunities for dealing with trading disputes by negotiation. The OECD also provides a forum for the consideration of issues related to economic development, such as the impact of industry on the environment.

CROSSING THE BORDER

The border between Mexico and the United States is one of the few places in the world where an economically highly developed country and a less economically developed one share a land boundary. This difference is reflected in the relationship between the two countries. The wealthier United States attracts immigrants from Mexico, many of whom are prepared to risk crossing the border illegally in search of work and a better quality of life. Although the large numbers of immigrants coming into the United States cause some problems, many of them provide a source of cheap labor and do menial jobs that no one else wants. Others may do skilled work or start their own businesses. People also move from the United States into Mexico, but more for recreation than work: over 80 percent of tourists visiting Mexico come from the United States. Manufactured goods cross the border

◀ Traders outside the Stock Market building in Mexico City. Mexico plays a very active role in global financial markets.

in both directions. Goods imported from Mexico tend to be cheaper than those produced in the United States because of the low Mexican wage rates. At the same time, the about thirty million better-off Mexicans buy goods imported from the United States and Canada.

FINANCIAL HELP

Despite the wealth generated by its oil and other exports, Mexico still needs money from the global community to tackle its problems of poverty. Mexico therefore receives international aid in the form of loans from the World Bank. In order to obtain funding and technical expertise for development programs, Mexico's government needs to work in cooperation with the World Bank and show a commitment to dealing with economic problems through its own development policies.

▶ A nodding-donkey oil well in Poza Rica. In addition to small onshore oil wells like this one, Mexico has huge offshore oil fields in the Gulf of Mexico.

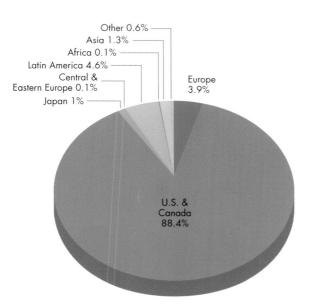

Other 0.6%
Asia 1.3%
Africa 0.1%
Latin America 4.6%
Central & Eastern Europe 0.1%
Japan 1%
Europe 3.9%
U.S. & Canada 88.4%

▲ Destination of exports by major trading region

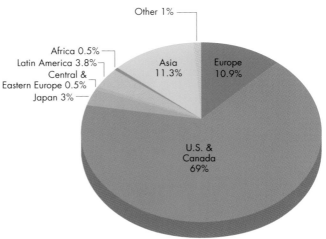

Other 1%
Africa 0.5%
Latin America 3.8%
Central & Eastern Europe 0.5%
Japan 3%
Asia 11.3%
Europe 10.9%
U.S. & Canada 69%

▲ Origin of imports by major trading region

PARTICIPATION IN THE INTERNATIONAL COMMUNITY

As a country with considerable biodiversity and an industrializing economy, Mexico faces many environmental protection issues. The country plays an important role in international environmental negotiations and has ratified more than one hundred international environmental agreements.

Mexico was one of the first countries to join the United Nations (UN), following its creation in 1945. As a member of the UN, Mexico is committed to working for world peace through international cooperation and respect for human rights. Mexico's government, however, has sometimes been guilty of human rights violations. During the 1970s and 1980s, for example, many left-wing opponents of the government mysteriously disappeared. When evidence from files kept by the security forces was made public in 2001, it showed that these activists were abducted, tortured, and killed. President Vicente Fox commissioned an investigation, and in 2002, three army officers were charged with murder. This was a step toward fulfilling a promise President Fox made when he was elected in 2000—to promote human rights and to increase Mexico's participation in international affairs.

? Did You Know?

Although Mexico has chosen not to become a member of the Organization of Petroleum Exporting Countries (OPEC), representatives of Mexico still attend most of OPEC's meetings. Mexico has also sometimes worked with OPEC to adjust world oil supplies. For example, in 2002, Mexico pledged to limit its oil exports to 1.66 million barrels per day—a cut of 100,000 barrels per day—for six months in order to stop oil prices from falling.

▼ All the main U.S. fast-food chains can be found in Mexico's cities. Individual street vendors, such as this one in Veracruz, are also influenced by the demand for American-style fast food.

A CULTURE UNDER THREAT?

Mexico and the United States have often been described as having a love-hate relationship. Some Mexicans are becoming concerned that aspects of American culture are starting to undermine Mexican traditions. For example, highly commercialized Halloween celebrations are threatening to replace Mexico's traditional Day of the Dead festivities. Likewise, American fast-food outlets, selling items such as burgers, hot dogs, pizza, and fries, are spreading into Mexico's towns and cities, and most films showing in Mexico's movie theaters are made in Hollywood. Mexico's cultural influence, however, has also spread beyond the country's borders. Mexican cuisine, for example has become one of the most popular foreign foods in developed countries such as the United States and Britain. Tex-Mex food, which comes from Mexican-American areas, incorporates influences from both sides of the border.

Focus on: The Mexican Film Industry

▲ Many Western movies have been filmed on the main street of Capuaderos, in Durango.

From the 1920s to the 1950s, Mexico had a thriving film industry, with its own studios and stars, that produced about 150 films a year. Since then, however, Mexico's film industry has faded away, and Hollywood has taken over. In 1998, only ten films were made in Mexico. This change has not only led to a loss of employment and status but also has made it difficult for Mexican film directors to portray the rich diversity of Mexico's society. Meanwhile, films made in Hollywood tend to stereotype Mexicans as poor, corrupt, and violent. In an attempt to revitalize Mexico's film industry, the country's Congress passed a law stating that 10 percent of Mexico's movie-theater screens must show Mexican-made films. Although the number of films made in Mexico rose to thirty in 2000, the country's film industry still does not have enough investment to enable it to recapture its former glory.

CHAPTER 9

Transportation and Communications

Mexico has the most extensive road network in Latin America. The quality of its roads, however, varies enormously. The number of paved roads in the country has increased considerably in recent years, rising from about 52,800 miles (85,000 km) in the mid-1990s to 67,165 miles (108,087 km) in 2002, although many of these roads are poorly maintained. Mexico's main highways, which link cities and cross into the United States, are usually of better quality and are used by freight trucks and inter-city buses as well as cars.

The Inter-American Highway, which is a section of the Pan-American Highway, runs 3,397 miles (5,470 km) down the country, from Nuevo Laredo on the U.S. border to Panama City, Panama. This highway links Mexico with Alaska, to the north, and Argentina, to the south, although it has a break of about 60 miles (97 km) south of Mexico.

▼ A busy highway in Monterrey. In Mexico, road transportation carries 95 percent of passenger traffic and 80 percent of freight.

TRAVELING BY RAIL, AIR, AND SEA

Mexico's railroad system is concentrated in the country's northern and central areas, though much of the country is too mountainous for railway track to be built. The country has numerous connections with the United States and a connection with Central American networks through Guatemala. Mexico's railroad system needs modernizing. Most of its rolling stock dates from the 1950s. Because of the rail network's inefficiency, few passengers use trains, and very little freight is carried by rail.

Mexico has 1,827 airports. Of these, 231 have paved runways and are able to handle large commercial aircraft. Mexico is the destination and starting point for many international flights, with growing numbers of passengers arriving and departing as the tourist industry expands. Mexican airports also handle many domestic flights.

The Mexican coastline has no natural harbors, but several ocean ports have been constructed. The east-coast ports include Veracruz, which is used for cargo; and Tampico, Coatzacoalcos,

and Progesso, which are used for petroleum. The main ports on the country's Pacific coast are Guaymas, Mazatlán, and Manzanillo. These ports used to be run by the state and had a reputation for inefficiency. Since 1993, when the ports were sold to private companies, an overall growth in freight, with 1.7 million containers handled nationally in 2003, has taken place. There country's coasts have several fishing ports, although 75 percent of Mexico's catch comes through ports on the Pacific coast.

 Did You Know?

One of the most scenic railroad routes in the world, the Chihuahua al Pacifico, runs from the United States, down through the Copper Canyon, to the Pacific coast. Work began on the line's construction in the 1870s. It has 86 tunnels and 37 bridges, and it was not completed until 1961. The line is now mainly used by tourists.

▼ A train station on the scenic line that runs through the Copper Canyon. Today, most of the line's passengers are sightseers.

TRANSPORTATION IN URBAN AND RURAL AREAS

Traffic congestion and air pollution caused by vehicle emissions are particularly pressing problems in Mexico City because of the huge number of people who live and work there. The city's subway system, opened in 1969, is one of the busiest in the world, with more than twelve million passengers using it every day. Car and bus use have outgrown the capacity of the city's roads, leading to almost continuous traffic jams. At any one time, more than five million drivers are attempting to drive their vehicles along the capital city's roads.

In rural areas, local buses are the most common form of transportation. Bicycles also provide an inexpensive way for people to move around. Some farmers have tractors, although most of these are old, and some farmers still depend on outdated forms of transportation such as donkey carts.

Transport and Communications

- 🗀 Total roads: 204,771 miles/329,532 km
- 🗀 Total paved roads: 67,165 miles/ 108,087 km
- 🗀 Total unpaved roads: 137,606 miles/ 221,445 km
- 🗀 Total railways: 12,116 miles/19,510 km
- 🗀 Major airports: 231
- 🗀 Cars per 1,000 people: 107
- 🗀 Mobile phones per 1,000 people: 255
- 🗀 Personal computers per 1,000 people: 82
- 🗀 Internet users per 1,000 people: 98

Sources: World Bank and CIA World Factbook

▼ Some people in Mexico use bicycles to carry passengers and parcels, as shown here in a photo taken in the Yucatán region.

Focus on: Air Quality in Mexico City

Mexico City's smog problem is particularly severe because most of its residents' vehicles are old and poorly maintained and because the city's location—in a valley with mountains on three sides—causes pollutants to become trapped in the air. To fight pollution, all cars have been equipped with catalytic converters. In addition, the city has "No Drive Days." These are days of the week on which vehicles with a particular digit at the end of their registration numbers are banned from entering the city. Some improvement in Mexico City's air has occurred, and it is now clear enough on most days to see the distant volcanoes. Ozone and suspended particles, however, still frequently reach levels that are considered to be a health hazard. Future plans include the development of a rapid transit bus system to encourage more people to use public transportation and leave their cars at home.

▼Heavy traffic in Mexico City. On smog alert days, schoolchildren are ordered to stay indoors.

MEDIA AND COMMUNICATIONS

As wealth has increased in northern and central Mexico, both radio and TV ownership have risen. Television was first introduced in the country in 1950; by the 1990s, more than 70 percent of the population had access to at least one TV set. Many people in Mexico listen to the radio, and the country has more than one thousand local and regional radio stations.

The number of telephone lines in Mexico increased from 8.7 million in 1995 to about 16 million in 2003. Businesses and government offices are now connected to the national telephone network, but many homes, particularly in poorer, rural neighborhoods, are not. Mobile phone use in Mexico is increasing quickly, with over 28 million users in 2003. Access to the Internet is also increasing, with over 10 million users in 2002. In addition, Mexico has international communications facilities, including satellite Earth stations and a high-capacity fiber-optic undersea cable linked to the United States, the Canary Islands, Spain, Morocco, and Italy.

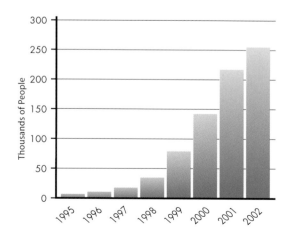

▲ Mobile phone use per 1,000 people, 1995–2002

CHAPTER 10

Education and Health

According to Mexico's constitution, children are guaranteed free education between the ages of six and fourteen. By 2008, this will be extended to include nursery school beginning at the age of three. While nearly all children in Mexico enroll in school, fewer than 90 percent complete primary education. Many wealthier Mexicans choose to pay for education, and about 10 percent of children attend private schools. Secondary education tends to focus on vocational and technical qualifications.

Universities, technical institutions, and teacher training colleges provide higher education in Mexico. The country has both public and private universities. Private ones, which are only open to those who can afford tuition, tend to have higher-quality facilities than public ones. Although they are poorly paid, teachers are generally highly regarded in Mexican society. In order to earn enough money, many teachers work two jobs. Some of them travel between two schools, while others take on evening work such as driving taxis.

OBSTACLES TO EDUCATION

School attendance of children from poor and isolated areas, many of whom are from indigenous groups, tends to be lower than the national average. This is because these children often go to work or because older children are needed at home to help with younger children. In addition, schools in these areas are not very well-equipped. Because of poor attendance and educational facilities, illiteracy among indigenous peoples is five times higher than the national average. In the state of Chiapas, for example, 23.5 percent of adults are illiterate, compared to Mexico City's rate of 3.1 percent. In the country as a whole, literacy rates have

◀ In the 1950s, the National Autonomous University of Mexico, located in Mexico City, moved to a campus. The campus includes this library, which is decorated with a mosaic by Juan O'Gorman that depicts Mexico's scientific achievements.

improved steadily, but the country still has a higher rate of literacy for men (92.6 percent) than for women (88.7 percent). Women in Mexico have traditionally been seen as homemakers, and this view still reduces access to education for many girls in the country. In the poorer urban areas of Mexico, the drop-out rate between the primary and secondary phases of education is high—as high as 66 percent in some places. This high drop-out rate is partly linked to a lack of job prospects.

Education and Health Data

- Life expectancy at birth, male: 70.7
- Life expectancy at birth, female: 76.7
- Infant mortality rate per 1,000: 24
- Under-five mortality rate per 1,000: 29
- Physicians per 1,000 people: 1.5
- Health expenditure as % of GDP: 6.1
- Education expenditure as % of GDP: 4.4
- Primary school net enrollment: 100%
- Student-teacher ratio, primary: 27.3
- Adult literacy % age 15+: 90.5

Sources: United Nations Agencies and World Bank

Did You Know?

In 1970, the average number of years a student in Mexico spent in school was four years for men and three years for women. By 2003, Mexico's average number of years in school had risen to eight years for men and seven years for women.

▼ These secondary school students from Los Mochis are fortunate enough to have access to good-quality educational resources.

THE HEALTH-CARE SYSTEM

Mexico's spending on health care is less than that of wealthier countries. For example, Mexico spends eight times less than the United States on health care. However, the number of doctors in the country has increased over the past ten years, and the basic public health system is used by 75 percent of the country's people. Higher-quality health care can be bought by the wealthy. There are also health-insurance programs for those employed in organizations and businesses, and Mexico's government plans to improve the public health-care system. Programs funded by the World Bank are targeting particular regions, mainly in the south of the country.

HEALTH ISSUES

Life expectancy in Mexico is relatively high. Many childhood diseases have been eradicated, and the infant mortality rate is now nationally about 24 per 1,000 live births. Mexico has a very effective childhood immunization program, with 95 percent of children being vaccinated against measles (compared to the United States's rate of 91 percent). In addition, 88 percent of Mexicans now have access to disinfected water, resulting in a decrease in gastrointestinal illnesses and the disappearance of cholera.

▼ A boy waits at a rural clinic in Chihuahua State. Rural areas in Mexico tend to have worse health-care facilities than towns and cities.

Not everyone, however, benefits equally from these measures. Indigenous groups usually live in rural and sometimes remote areas. They tend to have less access to health-care services and clean water and, therefore, suffer more health problems. Infant mortality is also more common among these groups. In the poorest areas in the southern states, the infant mortality rate is as high as 203 per 1,000 births, compared to 9 per 1,000 births in the richer parts of Mexico City.

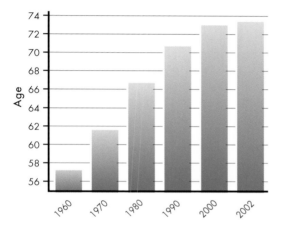

▲ Life expectancy at birth, 1960–2002

Rapidly growing urban areas, such as Mexico City and the northern industrial towns such as Ciudad Juarez, also have some neighborhoods that lack adequate water supplies and sanitation services. These urban areas also have poor air quality because of heavy concentrations of vehicles that emit pollutants. The result of this air pollution is a higher incidence of respiratory problems than in rural areas. It is thought that as many as one-third of Mexicans' respiratory problems are caused by air pollution.

► A Mayan Indian woman in Mérida. Groups such as the Maya are more likely to suffer from health problems caused by their poor living conditions.

Focus on: Lifestyle Health Problems

Diseases linked to a high-fat and high-sugar diet, such as heart disease and certain cancers, are becoming more common in Mexico. Adult obesity is also increasing. According to a report published in 2003, about 24 percent of Mexican adults were considered obese—a percentage higher than that of Britain but lower than that of the United States. This increase in obesity is likely to lead to a rise in diabetes in the next ten years. Obesity is increasing in Mexico partly because people's eating habits have changed as parts of the country have become wealthier. As is the case in many countries, fast food is now easily available and is often eaten instead of traditional foods. This can have damaging effects on health.

CHAPTER 11

Culture and Religion

Mexico has a very rich culture, reflecting its varied and eventful history that includes both ancient Mexican civilizations and Spanish colonization. The country has numerous examples of Mayan and Aztec architectural influences, especially in the colors and designs used to decorate buildings. Spanish influence is strong in the architecture of Mexico's central and southern regions, where many houses have an interior courtyard and wrought-iron grilles to protect the windows. Under Spanish rule, towns were planned with straight streets leading into a main square, or *plaza mayor*.

ART, MUSIC, AND FOOD

Mexico has a strong tradition of folk art and crafts, with particular regions specializing in different products, such as silver-work in central Mexico and hammocks from Yucatán. The country has many skilled wood-carvers, and wooden masks have been popular in the country since they were first used in the dances of ancient Mexico and later, in the sixteenth, seventeenth and eighteenth centuries, under Spanish rule. Painting has a long history in Mexico, and some Mexican painters have achieved worldwide fame. Perhaps the most widely known Mexican artist was Diego Rivera, a muralist who produced some of the greatest revolutionary art of the twentieth century between the 1920s and the 1950s. The two presidents who came to office after the Mexican Revolution, Alvaro Obregón (1920-1924) and Plutarco Calles (1924-1934), enlisted artists, including Rivera, to produce works that would portray the violence and heroism of the

▼ In the nineteenth century, mariachi bands played at weddings. Today, they are more often seen around Mexico playing for tourists.

Revolution. Rivera's huge murals, many of which are displayed in or on public buildings, depict the Mexican struggle for independence.

Like traditional Mexican art, traditional Mexican music also contains echoes from the country's past. Fiestas often include live music played on a range of instruments, such as the reed flute and conch shell, that originated in ancient Mexico. Meanwhile, stringed instruments, such as violins and guitars, were introduced to Mexico during the Spanish conquest. One of the best-known styles of music played with these stringed instruments is mariachi, which originated in Jalisco. Mariachi bands can consist of anywhere between four and fifteen members.

Mexican cuisine is very distinctive. It is the result of the mixing of cultures of the ancient

▲ Tacos are a traditional type of stuffed tortilla, made from maize or wheat flour.

civilizations, colonial Spain, and, more recently, influences from the United States. Corn, or maize, and two other widely used ingredients, beans and chilies, make up the basic diet for many Mexicans and have been staples since ancient times. The country has many regional variations in types of food and ways of cooking, but the use of corn in tortillas is common all over the country.

 Did You Know?

The ancient Mexican civilizations were the first to use both vanilla and chocolate. Vanilla and chocolate were introduced to other countries through trade.

▲ Families celebrate Independence Day together. These children in Mexico City are dressed up for the occasion.

THE FAMILY AND ITS TRADITIONS

Traditionally, the family has been the most important social institution in Mexican society. For many Mexicans, this is still the case today, although social attitudes are changing, particularly among those with the highest levels of income and education. The most significant changes in Mexican family life are those affecting the role of women. During the 1970s and 1980s, economic hardship required that more women in families work because their earnings were needed in addition to those of the male breadwinner. Since then, more women in Mexico have become economically independent. Many women now wish to have a role in society beyond that of the family unit. The changing role of women can sometimes conflict with machismo, the traditional code of behavior according to which Mexican men are expected to be strong, proud, and in control. An increasing number of Mexican men, however, want to be more involved in raising children.

RELIGIOUS BELIEFS AND PRACTICES

Most Mexicans are Catholic, the religion of the Spanish conquistadors. Their Catholicism is a distinctly Mexican form that merges traditional Catholic beliefs with beliefs from the religions of the ancient Mexican civilizations. One example of this is the Day of the Dead festival. Another example involves the Virgin of Guadalupe, the patron saint of Mexico. In 1531, an Indian peasant at Tepeyac, near Mexico City, saw a vision of a dark-skinned Virgin Mary who instructed him to build a shrine to her. The Aztec goddess Tonantzin had been worshiped at the same site, and many believed the peasant's vision to be the reappearance of this goddess. Each year, more than two million pilgrims visit this shrine on December 12.

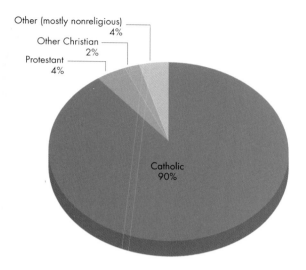

Other (mostly nonreligious)
4%

Other Christian
2%

Protestant
4%

Catholic
90%

▲ Mexico's major religions

▲ An eighteenth-century cathedral in Chihuahua.

Focus on: The Day of the Dead Festival

Every year, on the first two days of November, the people of Mexico remember their dead relatives in a festival called the Day of the Dead. The festivities vary from place to place, but all combine a sense of fun with a deeper spirituality. The souls of the dead are thought to visit their living relatives over these two days and are welcomed with special decorations, including skeletons and skulls made from papier mâché, chocolate, and sugar. Day of the Dead celebrations may also include candlelit processions to cemeteries. Elements of rituals from ancient religions and Christianity are included in the festivities; Aztec beliefs about Mictlantecuhtli, Lord of the Underworld, blend with the celebration of All Saints Day.

▲ People celebrating the Day of the Dead may wear skull masks and clothes with bones painted on them.

CHAPTER 12

Leisure and Tourism

Mexicans are enthusiastic about playing and watching a range of sports, and soccer is particularly popular. Mexico is the only country that has twice, in 1970 and 1986, hosted the World Cup finals. Another sport that is much-loved in Mexico is wrestling. Mexican wrestlers wear costumes and masks and take on names like *El Santo* (The Saint) or *El Vampiro* (The Vampire). Bullfighting is also very popular and has been part of Mexican culture for about five hundred years. Mexico has hundreds of bullrings, including the world's largest, in Mexico City, which can seat fifty thousand.

FAMILY AND HOME ENTERTAINMENT

Much leisure time in Mexico is spent among family members—either cooking and eating at home or going out together. Local celebrations also provide family entertainment, including fireworks, music, and dancing. Dancing is a popular leisure activity, and young children

▼ *Charrería* is the Mexican art of horseback riding. In charrería, riders demonstrate their skills on horseback in an arena similar to a bullring with mariachi music as accompaniment.

are taught social dances, such as merengue and salsa, at family fiestas. Numerous festivals take place throughout the year, and each one is celebrated with special foods and events. Some of these festivals are public holidays that mark significant historical and social events. For example, Cinco de Mayo commemorates Mexico's victory over France at Puebla in 1862. Other festivals, such as *Semana Santa* (Easter Week), are religious.

Many Mexicans spend much of their leisure time watching television, and some of the most popular programs in Mexico are the many soap operas *(telenovelas)*. The most successful of these can draw audiences of twenty-five million. They are made in Mexico, specifically for Mexican audiences, by the two main national broadcasters, Televisa and TV Azteca. Telenovela actors are celebrities in Mexican society and are often featured in magazines and newspaper gossip columns. In addition to magazines and newspapers, many Mexicans also enjoy reading *historieta*—pocket-sized comic books written for adult audiences.

▲ Mexico's tourist industry brings money into the country's economy, which can benefit people with small businesses, such as this shoeshiner in Guadalajara.

THE IMPACT OF TOURISM

Tourism is a major source of foreign earnings for Mexico, and it has become the largest source of employment in the country. Many jobs exist in tourist facilities, such as restaurants, hotels, golf courses, and scuba-diving businesses. Many more jobs are in small businesses, such as selling hand-made souvenirs at roadside stalls and cleaning shoes on city streets. About twenty million tourists a year visit Mexico. Most of them are from the United States, but Mexico's appeal is widening, and the country is now the eighth most popular vacation destination in the world. Opportunities for tourists in Mexico are very diverse. The country has luxurious, specially-built resort areas, such as Cancún, where accommodations, restaurants, shops, and leisure activities are all in one place. Visitors to Mexico can also take ecotourism trips and find facilities that cater to different tastes and budgets.

▲ The Acapulco divers are one of Mexico's most famous tourist attractions. Young men climb to the top of a cliff and dive into a narrow sea channel below. Timing is crucial, as the water is only deep enough when a wave swells through the channel.

Tourists come to Mexico for many reasons. Sandy beaches and warm seas, particularly along the Yucatán coast, appeal to those who want a beach vacation, while archaeological discoveries, such as those found at the Mayan site of Chichén Itzá, attract those with an interest in history and different cultures. Local customs and crafts, such as markets, dress, folk art, and jewelry-making, are also of interest to some tourists.

Mexico's varied physical environments, with their wide range of animal and plant species, attract ecotourists. For example, some tourists go into the mountainous interior of Baja California to spot bighorn sheep or visit the Pacific island of San Benito, which is a refuge for elephant seals. Recently, tourists have become increasingly interested in organized trips into wilderness areas, including hiking tours into the remote southwest of Tabasco.

Mexico's dependence on tourism for jobs and foreign revenue is risky. First, the tourist business is vulnerable to disruption by nature. The popular tourist resort of Acapulco, for example, was seriously damaged in 1997 by Hurricane Pauline. Government and city authorities made sure that Acapulco's tourist areas were cleaned up within a few weeks, but tourist figures were down by 15 percent six

Tourism in Mexico

- Tourist arrivals, millions: 19.667
- Earnings from tourism in U.S.$: 8,858,000,000
- Tourism as % foreign earnings: 5
- Tourist departures, millions: 11.948
- Expenditure on tourism in U.S.$: 6,060,000,000

Source: World Bank

months later—perhaps because tourists did not know about the speedy clean-up or were nervous about the risk of another hurricane. Other factors affecting the tourist industry include changes in the currency exchange rate and fear of terrorism. The number of American tourists visiting Mexico fell significantly for a couple of years after the September 11, 2001, attacks.

Focus on: Hot Springs and Spa Resorts

Because of Mexico's numerous volcanoes, the country has many places where hot mineral springs bubble up from underground. These springs provide mineral and spa baths that many people believe help tackle stress and health problems such as skin conditions. Evidence shows that wealthy Aztecs enjoyed these baths in ancient times. Many of Mexico's spas are quite simple— just a swimming pool filled with warm, murky brown mineral water—and are mostly used on weekends by Mexican families. Some spas, however, have luxury hotels for tourists.

▼ Some natural spas in Mexico, such as this one in Puebla, have been developed into major leisure attractions.

CHAPTER 13

Environment and Conservation

In Mexico, air pollution is a huge problem in industrial areas where companies have not been subject to emission controls and in large urban settlements with high levels of vehicle emissions. Ciudad Juárez, an industrial town on the Mexico-U.S. border, is one of the most affected places. More than one million trucks pass through the town every year, leaving high levels of suspended particles in the air. This type of pollution causes serious health problems, including asthma and respiratory disease, particularly among children.

The government has now brought in measures to tackle air pollution. These include tax incentives to encourage industries to buy pollution-control equipment. All gasoline sold by the national oil company, PEMEX, has been lead-free since 1998. In 2000, Mexico signed the Kyoto Protocol, an international treaty that aims to reduce greenhouse gas emissions. By 2004, Mexico had made some progress in slowing down the rate of increase in emissions, although it had not yet been able to significantly reduce the air pollution problem. Mexico's greenhouse gas emissions, however, are still well below those of highly industrialized countries and are the equivalent of those of the United States fifty years ago.

▼ Smog, which is caused by air pollution, hangs over Mexico City. Mexico's government is trying to reduce emissions from vehicles and industry.

Environmental and Conservation Data

📁 Forested area as % total land area: 29

📁 Protected area as % total land area: 5

📁 Number of protected areas: 150

SPECIES DIVERSITY

Category	Known species (1992–2002)	Threatened species (2002)
Mammals	491	70
Breeding birds	440	39
Reptiles	837	18
Amphibians	358	4
Fish	674	95
Plants	26,071	221

Source: World Resources Institute

PROBLEMS WITH WATER

Water pollution, often caused by the discharge of waste, is widespread in Mexico's urban and industrial areas. Only 25 percent of urban wastewater is treated, or cleaned of pollutants, and industrial wastewater is largely left untreated. The country's coastal waters also have problems. The Gulf of Mexico is affected by petroleum spills and also by untreated sewage, industrial waste, pesticides, and fertilizers that are washed into it. Mexico's government is building more treatment plants and raising awareness of the pollution problems, but it will take time for its water treatment measures to take effect. The aim is for 41 percent of urban wastewater and 15 percent of industrial wastewater to be treated by 2006. In the longer term, the goal is 60 percent overall wastewater treatment by 2025.

Another problem in Mexico is the over-exploitation of water supplies. As agriculture has become more intensive, farmers have needed to use more irrigation, and groundwater and rivers have become depleted, especially in the drier northern areas. Overuse of groundwater has also caused problems in Mexico City. The city is sited on an aquifer, or underground water source, from which water has been pumped to meet the rising demands of the huge population. As water has been removed, the sediments of the aquifer have become compressed, and the city has sunk about 33 feet (10 m) over the past century. In both the country's north and in Mexico City, attempts are now being made to use and transport water more efficiently in order to reduce demand.

 Did You Know?

The Rio Bravo/Rio Grande did not reach the sea in February 2001 because so much water had been used, mainly for irrigation, in the area of its drainage basin.

▲ Irrigation is used to grow over half of Mexico's agricultural produce, especially export crops such as the pecan nuts that grow on these trees.

BIODIVERSITY: THREATS AND PROTECTION

Mexico is classified as a megadiverse country, with 12 percent of the world's total biodiversity (animal and plant species). It also has one of the highest rates of deforestation in the world. About 770,000 acres (311,615 ha) of forest are cleared every year in order to rear livestock and cultivate crops. Although the government has pledged to reduce deforestation by 75 percent between 2001 and 2025, protected areas only made up 10 percent of the country's territory in 2003. Outside protected areas, it is far harder to prevent people from felling trees and destroying ecosystems. Positive national government initiatives have included the establishment of the National Commission for the Knowledge and Use of Biodiversity in 1992.

Mexico is also party to over one hundred international environmental agreements. Local and national projects have been set up under these agreements, including a sanctuary for gray whales, which are protected under the World

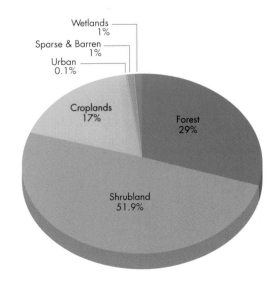

▲ Habitat type as percentage of total area

Heritage Convention. Mexico also participates in the Green Globe 21, an international sustainable tourism certification program set up following the 1992 Rio Earth Summit, a meeting at which many countries met to discuss how to tackle global environmental problems. To gain certification, tourist companies or resorts have to put principles of sustainability, such as water and energy conservation, into practice. Few have been fully certified, but many tourist enterprises are working toward it. In addition, with ecotourism depending on environmental attractions, Mexico has a strong commercial incentive to protect habitats, as well as an increased awareness of their global significance. Whale-watching trips off the coast of Baja California, for example, attract many tourists and also help ensure that the whales are protected.

THE GOAL OF SUSTAINABILITY

Sustainable development has become an explicit goal in Mexico's National Development Plan. Because of this goal, government funding is available for some environmental protection initiatives. World Bank loans have also been used to help Mexico balance economic development with sustainability through such initiatives as the Renewable Energy Program. This program promotes the development of wind and solar energy, sources of power for which Mexico has great potential.

▲ Monarch butterflies at the Monarch Butterfly Sanctuary in Michoacan. Every year, millions of monarchs make the 3,000 mile (4,827 km) trip between their winter roosts in central Mexico and their summer haunts in the United States.

Focus on: Recycling through "Scavenging"

Recycling of waste is an important aspect of sustainability. Currently, in Mexico, people known as "scavengers" work on urban landfills, making a living from selling recyclable materials they find there and also helping to improve Mexico's levels of sustainability. Working within the unhealthy conditions of landfill sites causes scavengers to have a high incidence of disease and a short life expectancy. If the authorities were to control and mechanize the retrieving of recyclable material, however, the scavengers would almost certainly lose their way of making a living. For these reasons, the scavengers are opposed to any regulation of waste recycling.

CHAPTER 14

Future Challenges

In the twenty-first century, Mexico faces a number of challenges. Economic development since World War II has given many people a better quality of life but there is concern that the pace of development in the country is not keeping up with population growth. Over 53 million people in Mexico have poor access to adequate basic services (clean water, sanitation, and electricity). With about 1.5 million new citizens every year, this situation is likely to worsen. Economic improvements in the country are unequally distributed, mainly benefiting the northern areas of the country and Mexico City, while the south remains poor. In addition, great poverty also exists in the urban slums and shantytowns of Mexico's cities and towns.

SUSTAINABLE DEVELOPMENT?

Finding a balance between economic development and protection of the environment is a challenge for Mexico that is the focus of recent initiatives funded by the World Bank. The Mexican government has also made sustainable development one of its highest priorities. Of the many environmental issues to be tackled, groundwater depletion and water shortage are causing particular concern. Demand for water is increasing because of population growth and economic development, especially the spread of more commercial forms

▼ Flamingos take flight in Celestun Nature Reserve. To protect the country's wildlife, Mexico's government has set up a number of nature reserves.

of agriculture, which require a lot of irrigation. In many areas, farmers are struggling with water shortages, and in the northern border area, water scarcity is also a source of friction between the United States and Mexico.

CROSS-BORDER ISSUES

Illegal immigration to the United States has a negative effect on Mexican settlements, which lose many young, economically active people. Both countries are adopting strategies to deal with this issue. For Mexico, these strategies include improving living conditions and increasing job opportunities so that people do not have to emigrate in search of a better quality of life.

Drug trafficking is another continuing cross-border issue. Heroin and cannabis originate from Mexican sources, and cocaine is smuggled through Mexico from areas further south. Mexico's government has drug-crop eradication programs in place, and these are seen as vital for tackling the problem.

MEXICAN NATIONAL IDENTITY

Some Mexicans are worried that their culture, with all its richness and diversity, will be lost or watered down in the face of increasing contact with ideas and practices from the United States. It is certainly true that Mexico has more fast food outlets than it did in the past, and more Hollywood movies are being shown in the country than used to be. However, a clear sense of national identity— underpinned by the concept of

Mexicanidad, or Mexican-ness—still exists in the country. Fundamental to this sense of identity are the influences of its ancient civilizations, awareness of European invasion and conquest, and the legacy of the struggles of the Mexican Revolution.

▼ Pancho Villa, one of the leaders of the Mexican Revolution, led his army from northern Mexico to fight against the dictatorship of Porfirio Diaz. Villa was assassinated in 1923, and about thirty thousand people attended his funeral.

Time Line

200 B.C.–A.D. 1200 Great urban civilizations, such as the Maya, Zapotecs, and Teotihuacán, develop.

1325 Aztecs settle in central Mexico.

1519 Hernán Cortés leads Spanish troops to Mexico in search of gold and silver.

1521–1821 Mexico is renamed New Spain and becomes a colony of Spain for three centuries.

1821 Mexico wins independence.

1824 Democratic federal republic of Mexico is established.

1876 General Porfirio Diaz seizes power and becomes the dictator of Mexico.

1910–1917 Mexican Revolution to overthrow dictatorship and establish rights of all citizens.

1917 Present-day Mexican Constitution drawn up.

1942 Mexico declares war on Japan and Germany in World War II.

1945 Mexico joins the United Nations.

1950 Television introduced in Mexico.

1954 Mexican women gain the right to vote.

1968 Mexico hosts the Olympic Games.

Government troops open fire on a student demonstration, killing hundreds.

1969 Subway opens in Mexico City.

1970 Mexico hosts the finals of the World Cup soccer match. (It hosts again in 1986.)

1981 Oil prices drop, leaving Mexico unable to repay foreign loans.

1985 Mexico City hit by earthquake measuring 8.1 on Richter scale. Over 20,000 are killed.

1994 Mexico joins the United States and Canada in the North American Free Trade Agreement (NAFTA); Uprising of Indians in the Chiapas region of Mexico takes place.

1998 Closure of the world's biggest silver mine at Real de Angeles.

2000 Vicente Fox, of the National Action Party, is elected president of Mexico, ending seventy years of domination by the Partido Revolucionario Institucional.

Volcano Popocatépetl, near Mexico City, erupts for the first time since the 1920s.

2001 The Zapatista National Liberation Army, representing the Indians in Chiapas region, stages a two-week march to Mexico City calling for Mexico's congress to approve a bill on Indian rights.

Glossary

altitude the height of the land above sea level, sometimes known as elevation

aquifer an underground source of water where rainwater has seeped into a layer of porous rock.

biodiversity variety of forms of life

constitution a document that sets out the basic principles and laws on which a government is based

coup a sudden, often violent, overthrowing of a government

deputy an elected representative in the Chamber of Deputies of Mexico's federal government, whose job it is to debate and help decide whether to pass particular laws

dictatorship a form of government in which the ruler, or dictator, has complete power

federal republic a type of government under which a country has both a national government and state governments beneath it

greenhouse gases gases in Earth's atmosphere, such as carbon dioxide, methane, and nitrous oxides, that trap the heat from the sun in the atmosphere

gross domestic product (GDP) the total value of goods and services produced within the borders of a country

gross national income (GNI) the total value of a country's income from goods and services produced by its residents both within the country and elsewhere in the world

illiterate unable to read or write

independence the state of being able to control one's own affairs

indigenous people the original or native population who first lived in an area or country

infrastructure the basic system of public works in a country, state, or region, such as roads, railroads, electricity, and phone lines, necessary for a society to function

mariachi music traditional Mexican music originating in the eighteenth century and played by a small band, usually including a guitarist, violinist, and trumpeter.

maquiladora a factory, usually located near the Mexico-U.S. border, in which goods mainly intended for sale in the United States are produced using inexpensive Mexican labor

National Congress the branch of Mexico's government, made up of the Senate and the Chamber of Deputies, in which the country's laws are made

rapid transit system a public transport system, such as a bus or rail system, designed to carry large numbers of people as quickly as possible in large congested urban areas

reservoirs places where water is collected and stored

scavenger in Mexico, a person who makes his or her living by finding items and materials dumped in landfills that can be sold for recycling

seismic activity earthquakes and volcanic eruptions

senator an elected member of the Senate (which is part of the federal government), who helps decide on the laws of the country

shantytown a collection of temporary dwellings made of scrap materials and built on the edges of cities in less developed countries by people with little or no income

sisal fiber produced from the leaves of a plant and used to make rope.

sustainable development economic development that can be continued without damaging the environment

tectonic area a region affected by earthquakes and volcanoes triggered by movements of the large sections of Earth's crust known as tectonic plates

tsunami a very large ocean wave caused by an earthquake or volcanic eruption beneath the sea

wastewater treatment removal of pollutants and harmful substances from water that has been used in households or by industries

Further Information

BOOKS TO READ

Aztec (Native American Peoples series)
Mary Stout
(Gareth Stevens Publishing)

*Diego Rivera (Checkerboard Biography
Library series)*
Joanne Mattern
(ABDO)

*Emiliano Zapata (Proud Heritage:
The Hispanic Library series)*
R. Conrad Stein
(Child's World)

Mexico (Countries of the World series)
Edward Parker
(Facts on File)

Mexico (World of Recipes series)
Julie McCulloch
(Heinemann)

Mexico City (Great Cities of the World series)
Marion Morrison
(World Almanac Library)

*Mystery of the Maya: Uncovering
the Lost City of Palenque*
Peter Lourie
(Boyds Mills Press)

The Rio Grande (Rivers of North America series)
Kathleen Fahey
(Gareth Stevens Publishing)

USEFUL WEB SITES

Beyond the Border
www.pbs.org/itvs/beyondtheborder

Discovering Mexico
www.nationalgeographic.com/mexico/

Earth Trends
www.earthtrends.org

Global Tribe: Mexico
www.pbs.org/kcet/globaltribe/countries/
mex_journal.html

Mexico for Kids
www.elbalero.gob.mx/kids

Monarch Watch
www.monarchwatch.org

Oaxaca
www.questconnect.org/Oaxaca_Mexico.htm

World Almanac for Kids Online: Mexico
www.worldalmanacforkids.com/explore/nation
s/mexico.html

The World Factbook
www.odci.gov/cia/publications/factbook/
geos/mx.html

Xcaret
www.xcaret.com/indexxc.php

Index

Page numbers in **bold**
indicate pictures.